SOUND INNOVATIONS

ENSEMBLE DEVELOPMENT

Chorales and Warm-up Exercises for Tone, Technique and Rhythm

INTERMEDIATE CONCERT BAND

Peter **BOONSHAFT** | Chris **BERNOTAS**

Thank you for making *Sound Innovations: Ensemble Development* a part of your concert band curriculum. With 412 exercises, including over 70 chorales by some of today's most renowned composers for concert band, it is our hope you will find this book to be a valuable resource in helping you grow in your understanding and abilities as an ensemble musician.

An assortment of exercises are grouped by key and presented in a variety of intermediate difficulty levels. Where possible, several exercises in the same category are provided to allow for variety while accomplishing the goals of that specific type of exercise. You will notice that many exercises and chorales are clearly marked with dynamics, articulations, style, and tempo for you to practice those aspects of performance. Other exercises are intentionally left for you or your teacher to determine how best to use them in reaching your performance goals.

Whether you are progressing through exercises to better your technical facility or to challenge your musicianship with beautiful chorales, we are confident you will be excited, motivated, and inspired by using *Sound Innovations: Ensemble Development*.

© 2012 Alfred Music Publishing Co., Inc.
Sound Innovations™ is a trademark of Alfred Music Publishing Co., Inc.
All Rights Reserved including Public Performance

ISBN-10: 0-7390-6770-2
ISBN-13: 978-0-7390-6770-3

Instrument photos courtesy of Yamaha Corporation of America Band & Orchestral Division

Concert B♭ Major (Your C Major)

1 PASSING THE TONIC

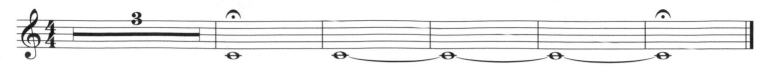

2 PASSING THE TONIC

3 PASSING THE TONIC

4 PASSING THE TONIC

5 PASSING THE TONIC

6 BREATHING AND LONG TONES

7 BREATHING AND LONG TONES

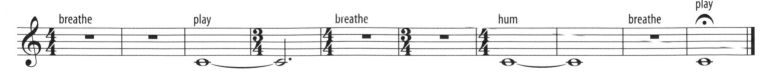

8 BREATHING AND LONG TONES

9 BREATHING AND LONG TONES

10 CONCERT B♭ MAJOR SCALE (YOUR C MAJOR SCALE)

11 SCALE PATTERN

12 SCALE PATTERN

13 SCALE PATTERN

14 SCALE PATTERN

15 SCALE PATTERN

16 CHANGING SCALE RHYTHM

17 CONCERT B♭ CHROMATIC SCALE (YOUR C CHROMATIC SCALE)

4

18 FLEXIBILITY

19 FLEXIBILITY

20 ARPEGGIOS

21 ARPEGGIOS

22 INTERVALS

23 INTERVALS

24 BALANCE AND INTONATION: PERFECT INTERVALS

25 BALANCE AND INTONATION: DIATONIC HARMONY

26 BALANCE AND INTONATION: FAMILY BALANCE

5

27 BALANCE AND INTONATION: LAYERED TUNING

28 BALANCE AND INTONATION: MOVING CHORD TONES

29 BALANCE AND INTONATION: SHIFTING CHORD QUALITIES

30 EXPANDING INTERVALS: DOWNWARD IN PARALLEL OCTAVES

31 EXPANDING INTERVALS: DOWNWARD IN PARALLEL FIFTHS

32 EXPANDING INTERVALS: DOWNWARD IN TRIADS

33 EXPANDING INTERVALS: UPWARD IN PARALLEL OCTAVES

34 EXPANDING INTERVALS: UPWARD IN TRIADS

35 RHYTHM

6

36 RHYTHM

37 RHYTHM

38 RHYTHM

39 RHYTHM

40 RHYTHMIC SUBDIVISION

41 RHYTHMIC SUBDIVISION

42 RHYTHMIC SUBDIVISION

43 METER

44 **PHRASING**

45 **PHRASING**

46 **ARTICULATION**

47 **DYNAMICS**

48 **ETUDE**

49 **ETUDE**

50 CHORALE: JESU, MEINE ZUVERSICHT

Johann Cruger (1598–1662)
Arranged by Todd Stalter

51 CHORALE

Michael Story (ASCAP)

52 CONCERT B♭ MAJOR SCALE & CHORALE

Chris M. Bernotas (ASCAP)

53 CHORALE

Chris M. Bernotas (ASCAP)

54 CHORALE

Randall D. Standridge (ASCAP)

55 CHORALE

Andrew Boysen, Jr.

10

Concert G Minor (Your A Minor)

61 PASSING THE TONIC

62 BREATHING AND LONG TONES

63 CONCERT G NATURAL MINOR SCALE (YOUR A NATURAL MINOR SCALE)

64 CONCERT G HARMONIC AND MELODIC MINOR SCALES

65 SCALE PATTERN

66 CONCERT G CHROMATIC SCALE (YOUR A CHROMATIC SCALE)

67 FLEXIBILITY

68 FLEXIBILITY

69 ARPEGGIOS

70 **ARPEGGIOS**

71 **INTERVALS**

72 **INTERVALS**

73 **BALANCE AND INTONATION: DIATONIC HARMONY**

74 **BALANCE AND INTONATION: MOVING CHORD TONES**

75 **BALANCE AND INTONATION: LAYERED TUNING**

76 **BALANCE AND INTONATION: FAMILY BALANCE**

77 **EXPANDING INTERVALS: DOWNWARD IN PARALLEL FIFTHS**

78 **EXPANDING INTERVALS: UPWARD IN PARALLEL THIRDS**

79 **RHYTHM**

80 **RHYTHM**

81 **RHYTHM**

82 **RHYTHMIC SUBDIVISION**

83 **RHYTHMIC SUBDIVISION**

84 **ARTICULATION AND DYNAMICS**

85 **ETUDE**

86 CHORALE — Larghetto — Robert Sheldon

87 CHORALE — Moderato — Michael Story (ASCAP)

88 G MINOR SCALE & CHORALE — Chris M. Bernotas (ASCAP)

89 CHORALE — Moderately slow, smoothly — Andrew Boysen, Jr.

90 CHORALE — Sad and expressive, freely — Rossano Galante

14

Concert E♭ Major (Your F Major)

91 **PASSING THE TONIC**

92 **PASSING THE TONIC**

93 **PASSING THE TONIC**

94 **PASSING THE TONIC**

95 **PASSING THE TONIC**

96 **BREATHING AND LONG TONES**

97 **BREATHING AND LONG TONES**

98 **BREATHING AND LONG TONES**

99 **BREATHING AND LONG TONES**

100 CONCERT E♭ MAJOR SCALE (YOUR F MAJOR SCALE)

101 SCALE PATTERN

102 SCALE PATTERN

103 SCALE PATTERN

104 SCALE PATTERN

105 SCALE PATTERN

106 CHANGING SCALE RHYTHM

107 CONCERT E♭ CHROMATIC SCALE (YOUR F CHROMATIC SCALE)

108 FLEXIBILITY

109 FLEXIBILITY

110 ARPEGGIOS

111 ARPEGGIOS

112 INTERVALS

113 INTERVALS

114 BALANCE AND INTONATION: PERFECT INTERVALS

115 BALANCE AND INTONATION: DIATONIC HARMONY

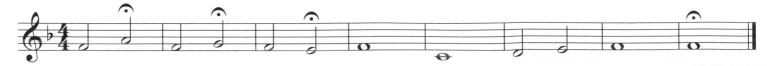

116 BALANCE AND INTONATION: FAMILY BALANCE

117 BALANCE AND INTONATION: LAYERED TUNING

118 BALANCE AND INTONATION: LAYERED TUNING

119 BALANCE AND INTONATION: SHIFTING CHORD QUALITIES

120 EXPANDING INTERVALS: DOWNWARD IN PARALLEL OCTAVES

121 EXPANDING INTERVALS: DOWNWARD IN PARALLEL FIFTHS

122 EXPANDING INTERVALS: DOWNWARD IN TRIADS

123 EXPANDING INTERVALS: UPWARD IN PARALLEL OCTAVES

124 EXPANDING INTERVALS: UPWARD IN TRIADS

125 RHYTHM

126 RHYTHM

127 RHYTHM

128 RHYTHM

129 RHYTHM

130 RHYTHMIC SUBDIVISION

131 RHYTHMIC SUBDIVISION

132 RHYTHMIC SUBDIVISION

19

133 METER

134 PHRASING

135 PHRASING

136 ARTICULATION

137 DYNAMICS

138 ETUDE

139 ETUDE

20

145 **CHORALE**

Andante

Robert Sheldon

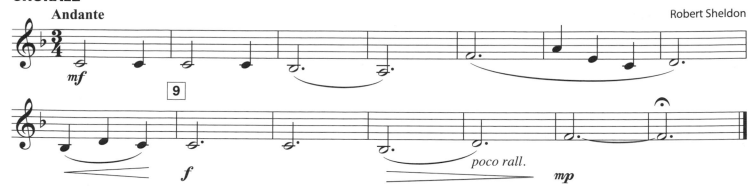

146 **CHORALE**

Solemnly

Ralph Ford (ASCAP)

147 **CHORALE**

Molto espressivo

Rossano Galante

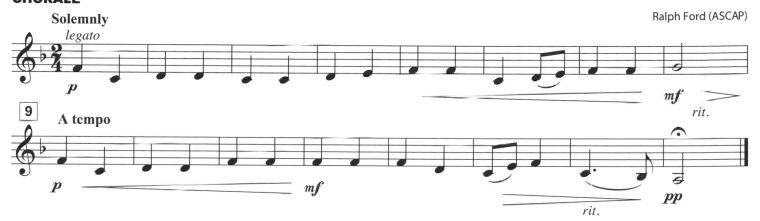

148 **CHORALE**

Adagio

Chris M. Bernotas (ASCAP)

149 **CHORALE**

Randall D. Standridge (ASCAP)

Concert C Minor (Your D Minor)

150 PASSING THE TONIC

151 BREATHING AND LONG TONES

152 CONCERT C NATURAL MINOR SCALE (YOUR D NATURAL MINOR SCALE)

153 CONCERT C HARMONIC AND MELODIC MINOR SCALES

154 SCALE PATTERN

155 CONCERT C CHROMATIC SCALE (YOUR D CHROMATIC SCALE)

156 FLEXIBILITY

157 FLEXIBILITY

23

158 ARPEGGIOS

159 ARPEGGIOS

160 INTERVALS

161 INTERVALS

162 BALANCE AND INTONATION: DIATONIC HARMONY

163 BALANCE AND INTONATION: MOVING CHORD TONES

164 BALANCE AND INTONATION: LAYERED TUNING

165 BALANCE AND INTONATION: FAMILY BALANCE

166 EXPANDING INTERVALS: DOWNWARD IN TRIADS

167 EXPANDING INTERVALS: UPWARD IN TRIADS

168 RHYTHM

169 RHYTHM

170 RHYTHM

171 RHYTHMIC SUBDIVISION

172 RHYTHMIC SUBDIVISION

173 ARTICULATION AND DYNAMICS

174 ETUDE

175 CHORALE

Randall D. Standridge (ASCAP)

176 CHORALE

Roland Barrett

177 CONCERT C MINOR SCALE & CHORALE

Chris M. Bernotas (ASCAP)

178 CHORALE: MEINES LEBENS LETZTE ZEIT

From the Gotha Psalter, 1726
Harmonized by J.S. Bach (1685–1750)
Arranged by Todd Stalter

179 CHORALE

Rossano Galante

26

Concert F Major (Your G Major)

180 PASSING THE TONIC

181 BREATHING AND LONG TONES

182 CONCERT F MAJOR SCALE (YOUR G MAJOR SCALE)

183 SCALE PATTERN

184 SCALE PATTERN

185 CONCERT F CHROMATIC SCALE (YOUR G CHROMATIC SCALE)

186 FLEXIBILITY

187 FLEXIBILITY

188 ARPEGGIOS

189 ARPEGGIOS

190 INTERVALS

191 BALANCE AND INTONATION: DIATONIC HARMONY

192 BALANCE AND INTONATION: FAMILY BALANCE

193 BALANCE AND INTONATION: LAYERED TUNING

194 BALANCE AND INTONATION: MOVING CHORD TONES

195 BALANCE AND INTONATION: SHIFTING CHORD QUALITIES

196 EXPANDING INTERVALS: DOWNWARD IN PARALLEL FIFTHS

197 EXPANDING INTERVALS: UPWARD IN PARALLEL FIFTHS

198 RHYTHM

199 RHYTHM

200 RHYTHM

201 RHYTHMIC SUBDIVISION

202 RHYTHMIC SUBDIVISION

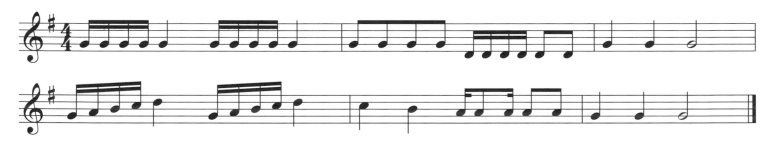

203 ARTICULATION AND DYNAMICS

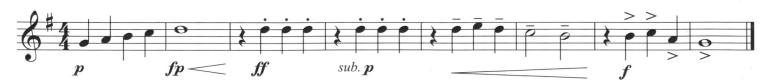

204 ETUDE

205 **CHORALE: OVERTURE 1812**

Pyotr Ilyich Tchaikovsky
Arranged by Michael Story (ASCAP)

206 **CHORALE**

Randall D. Standridge (ASCAP)

207 **CONCERT F MAJOR SCALE & CHORALE**

Chris M. Bernotas (ASCAP)

208 **CHORALE**

Rossano Galante

209 **CHORALE**

Ralph Ford (ASCAP)

Concert D Minor (Your E Minor)

210 PASSING THE TONIC

211 BREATHING AND LONG TONES

212 CONCERT D NATURAL MINOR SCALE (YOUR E NATURAL MINOR SCALE)

213 CONCERT D HARMONIC AND MELODIC MINOR SCALES

214 SCALE PATTERN

215 SCALE PATTERN

216 CONCERT D CHROMATIC SCALE (YOUR E CHROMATIC SCALE)

217 FLEXIBILITY

218 FLEXIBILITY

219 ARPEGGIOS

220 ARPEGGIOS

221 INTERVALS

222 BALANCE AND INTONATION: DIATONIC HARMONY

223 BALANCE AND INTONATION: FAMILY BALANCE

224 BALANCE AND INTONATION: LAYERED TUNING

225 BALANCE AND INTONATON: MOVING CHORD TONES

226 EXPANDING INTERVALS: DOWNWARD IN TRIADS

227 EXPANDING INTERVALS: UPWARD IN TRIADS

228 **RHYTHM**

229 **RHYTHM**

230 **RHYTHM**

231 **RHYTHMIC SUBDIVISION**

232 **RHYTHMIC SUBDIVISION**

233 **ARTICULATION AND DYNAMICS**

234 **ETUDE**

Concert A♭ Major (Your B♭ Major)

240 **PASSING THE TONIC**

241 **BREATHING AND LONG TONES**

242 **CONCERT A♭ MAJOR SCALE (YOUR B♭ MAJOR SCALE)**

243 **SCALE PATTERN**

244 **SCALE PATTERN**

245 **CONCERT A♭ CHROMATIC SCALE (YOUR B♭ CHROMATIC SCALE)**

246 **FLEXIBILITY**

247 **FLEXIBILITY**

248 ARPEGGIOS

249 ARPEGGIOS

250 INTERVALS

251 BALANCE AND INTONATION: DIATONIC HARMONY

252 BALANCE AND INTONATION: FAMILY BALANCE

253 BALANCE AND INTONATION: LAYERED TUNING

254 BALANCE AND INTONATION: MOVING CHORD TONES

255 EXPANDING INTERVALS: DOWNWARD IN PARALLEL FIFTHS

256 EXPANDING INTERVALS: UPWARD IN PARALLEL THIRDS

265 **CHORALE**

Randall D. Standridge (ASCAP)

266 **CHORALE**

Andrew Boysen, Jr.

267 **CONCERT A♭ MAJOR SCALE & CHORALE**

Chris M. Bernotas (ASCAP)

268 **CHORALE**

Ralph Ford (ASCAP)

269 **CHORALE**

Roland Barrett

Concert F Minor (Your G Minor)

270 **PASSING THE TONIC**

271 **BREATHING AND LONG TONES**

272 **CONCERT F NATURAL MINOR SCALE (YOUR G NATURAL MINOR SCALE)**

273 **CONCERT F HARMONIC AND MELODIC MINOR SCALES**

274 **SCALE PATTERN**

275 **CONCERT F CHROMATIC SCALE (YOUR G CHROMATIC SCALE)**

276 **FLEXIBILITY**

277 **FLEXIBILITY**

278 **ARPEGGIOS**

279 ARPEGGIOS

280 INTERVALS

281 INTERVALS

282 BALANCE AND INTONATION: DIATONIC HARMONY

283 BALANCE AND INTONATION: FAMILY BALANCE

284 BALANCE AND INTONATION: LAYERED TUNING

285 BALANCE AND INTONATION: MOVING CHORD TONES

286 EXPANDING INTERVALS: DOWNWARD IN TRIADS

287 EXPANDING INTERVALS: UPWARD IN TRIADS

288 **RHYTHM**

289 **RHYTHM**

290 **RHYTHM**

291 **RHYTHMIC SUBDIVISION**

292 **RHYTHMIC SUBDIVISION**

293 **ARTICULATION AND DYNAMICS**

294 **ETUDE**

295 CHORALE

Randall D. Standridge (ASCAP)

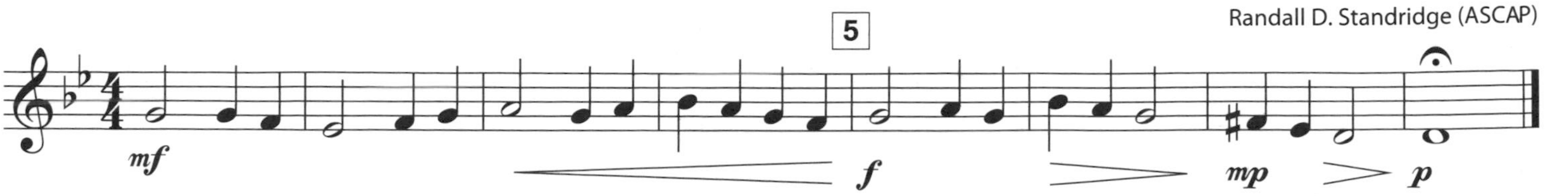

296 CHORALE

Roland Barrett

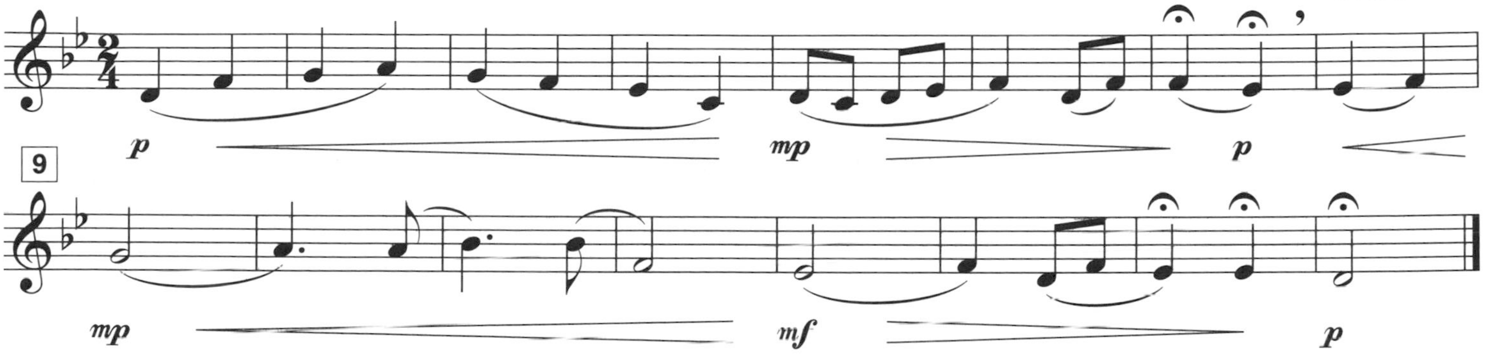

297 CONCERT F MINOR SCALE & CHORALE

Chris M. Bernotas (ASCAP)

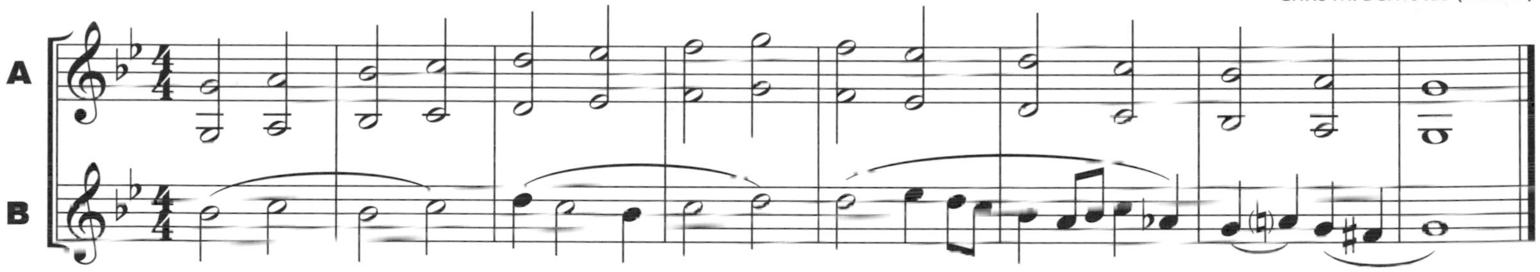

A

B

298 CHORALE

Robert Sheldon

Andante

299 CHORALE

Ralph Ford (ASCAP)

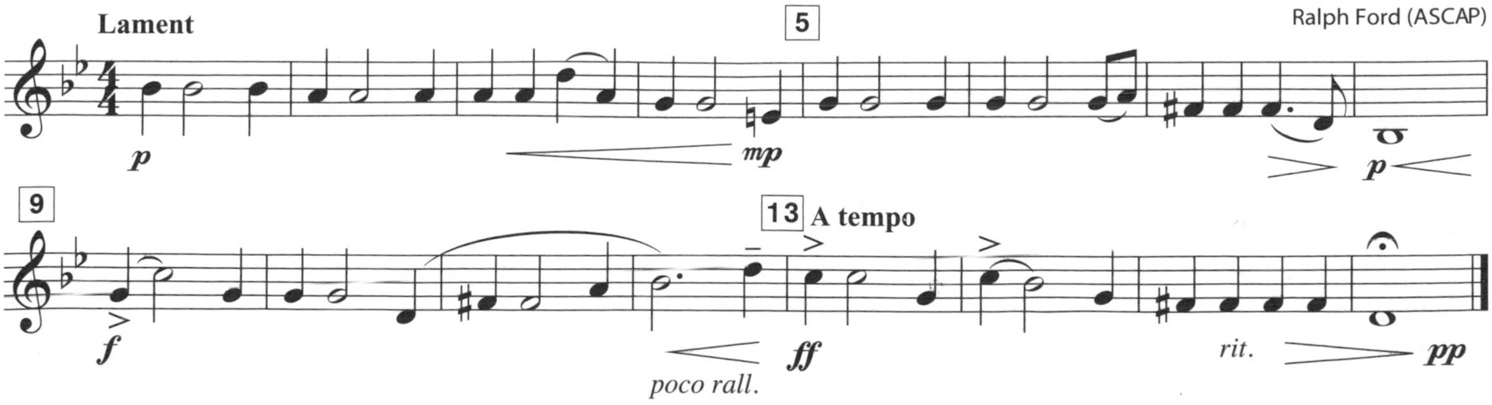

Lament

A tempo

Concert D♭ Major (Your E♭ Major)

300 BREATHING AND LONG TONES

301 CONCERT D♭ MAJOR SCALE (YOUR E♭ MAJOR SCALE)

302 SCALE PATTERN

303 SCALE PATTERN

304 SCALE PATTERN

305 FLEXIBILITY

306 ARPEGGIOS

307 INTERVALS

308 BALANCE AND INTONATION: FAMILY BALANCE

309 BALANCE AND INTONATION: LAYERED TUNING

310 EXPANDING INTERVALS: DOWNWARD AND UPWARD IN PARALLEL OCTAVES

311 ARTICULATION AND DYNAMICS

312 ETUDE

313 ETUDE

314 CHORALE

Andrew Boysen, Jr.

315 CHORALE

Todd Stalter

Concert B♭ Minor (Your C Minor)

316 BREATHING AND LONG TONES

317 CONCERT B♭ NATURAL MINOR SCALE (YOUR C NATURAL MINOR SCALE)

318 CONCERT B♭ HARMONIC AND MELODIC MINOR SCALES

319 SCALE PATTERN

320 SCALE PATTERN

321 FLEXIBILITY

322 ARPEGGIOS

323 INTERVALS

324 BALANCE AND INTONATION: LAYERED TUNING

325 **BALANCE AND INTONATION: MOVING CHORD TONES**

326 **EXPANDING INTERVALS: DOWNWARD IN TRIADS**

327 **ARTICULATION AND DYNAMICS**

328 **ETUDE**

329 **ETUDE**

330 **CHORALE**

Michael Story (ASCAP)

331 **CHORALE**

Robert Sheldon

Concert C Major (Your D Major)

332 BREATHING AND LONG TONES

333 CONCERT C MAJOR SCALE (YOUR D MAJOR SCALE)

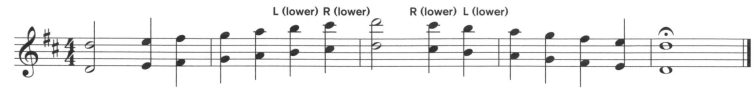

334 SCALE PATTERN

335 SCALE PATTERN

336 FLEXIBILITY

337 ARPEGGIOS

338 INTERVALS

339 INTERVALS

340 BALANCE AND INTONATION: FAMILY BALANCE

341 BALANCE AND INTONATION: LAYERED TUNING

342 EXPANDING INTERVALS: DOWNWARD IN PARALLEL FIFTHS

343 ARTICULATION AND DYNAMICS

344 ETUDE

Stately

345 ETUDE

346 CHORALE

Ralph Ford (ASCAP)

Flowingly

347 CHORALE: LARGO FROM THE "NEW WORLD SYMPHONY"

Antonín Dvořák
Arranged by Michael Story (ASCAP)

Andante

48

Concert A Minor (Your B Minor)

348 **BREATHING AND LONG TONES**

349 **CONCERT A NATURAL MINOR SCALE (YOUR B NATURAL MINOR SCALE)**

350 **CONCERT A HARMONIC AND MELODIC MINOR SCALES**

351 **SCALE PATTERN**

352 **FLEXIBILITY**

353 **ARPEGGIOS**

354 **INTERVALS**

355 **INTERVALS**

356 **BALANCE AND INTONATION: DIATONIC HARMONY**

357 BALANCE AND INTONATION: FAMILY BALANCE

358 EXPANDING INTERVALS: DOWNWARD IN TRIADS

359 ARTICULATION AND DYNAMICS

360 ETUDE

Slowly, with feeling

361 ETUDE

Moderately

362 CHORALE

Adagio

Todd Stalter

363 CHORALE

Roland Barrett

50

Concert G Major (Your A Major)

364 CONCERT G MAJOR SCALE (YOUR A MAJOR SCALE)

L (upper) R (upper) R (upper) L (upper)

365 BALANCE AND INTONATION: FAMILY BALANCE

366 ETUDE

Andante

pp $<$ $<$ f $>$ mf rit. pp

367 CHORALE

Moderately slow   5   Michael Story (ASCAP)

mf rit.

Concert E Minor (Your F# Minor)

368 CONCERT E NATURAL MINOR SCALE (YOUR F# NATURAL MINOR SCALE)

L (lower)

369 CONCERT E HARMONIC AND MELODIC MINOR SCALES

harmonic minor scale   CH. (upper)   melodic minor scale R (upper)

CH.

L (lower)

370 BALANCE AND INTONATION: LAYERED TUNING

371 ETUDE

Mournfully

mf $<$ f $>$ mf dim. mp

372 CHORALE

Slowly   5   Chris M. Bernotas (ASCAP)

mf $<$ f $>$ mp

Advancing Rhythm and Meter

52

383 $\frac{6}{8}$ **METER**

384 $\frac{6}{8}$ **METER**

385 $\frac{6}{8}$ **METER**

386 $\frac{6}{8}$ **METER**

387 $\frac{6}{8}$ **METER**

388 $\frac{6}{8}$ **METER**

389 $\frac{6}{8}$ **METER**

390 $\frac{6}{8}$ **METER**

391 **CHANGING METERS:** $\frac{4}{4}$ **AND** $\frac{6}{8}$

392 **CHANGING METERS:** $\frac{3}{4}$ **AND** $\frac{6}{8}$

393 **TRIPLETS**

394 **TRIPLETS**

395 **TRIPLETS**

396 **TRIPLETS**

397 **TRIPLETS**

398 **TRIPLETS**

399 **TRIPLETS**

400 **TRIPLETS**

401 **TRIPLETS**

402 **TRIPLETS**

54

403 $\frac{3}{8}$ METER

404 $\frac{3}{8}$ METER

405 $\frac{9}{8}$ METER

406 $\frac{9}{8}$ METER

407 $\frac{12}{8}$ METER

408 $\frac{12}{8}$ METER

409 $\frac{5}{8}$ METER

410 $\frac{5}{8}$ METER

411 $\frac{7}{8}$ METER

412 $\frac{7}{8}$ METER

Clarinet Fingering Chart

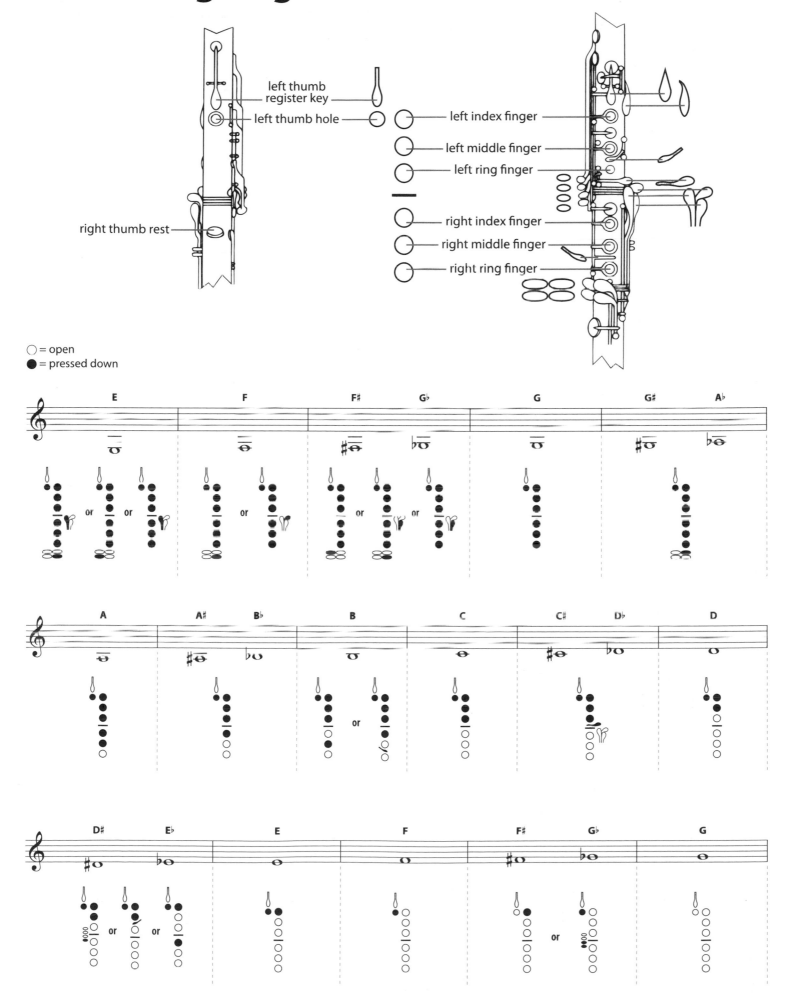

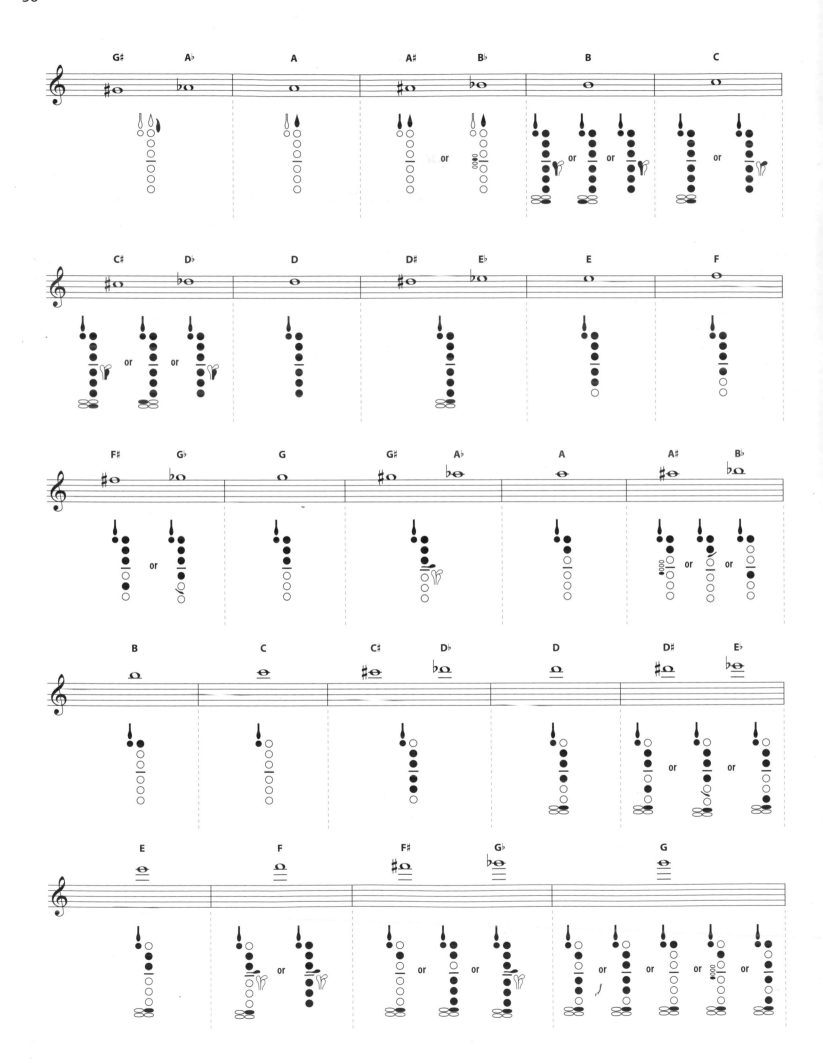